Hymns
in
Today's Language?

by

Christopher Idle

Rector of Limehouse, London E14

GROVE BOOKS

BRAMCOTE   NOTTS.

CONTENTS

NOTE

This booklet is largely the fruit of a 'group mind' which has grown up over some eight years of working together on the Words Committee of *Hymns for Today's Church*—which last year became part of a new enterprise, 'Jubilate Hymns'. In particular, it owes a great deal to the stimulus, writing, criticism, and friendship of Michael Perry, and the wise and unruffled chairmanship of Michael Saward. Within the group, strong opposites were frequently expressed, and I alone am responsible for the views and conclusions set down here. But my special thanks go to the other group members, notably the two Michaels; to Robin Leaver who (like them) read the draft and made some valuable suggestions; to Mrs. Ann Darlington and Mrs. Bunty Grundy for their generous secretarial help; and to my wife and family for providing their wholehearted support during six hard years and two impossible ones.

Christopher Idle

Abbreviations

AHB	*Anglican Hymn Book* (1965)
AMR	*Hymns Ancient and Modern,* (Revised edition, 1950)
EH	*The English Hymnal* (1906)

First impression July 1982

ISSN 0144–1728

ISBN 0 907536 27 1

PREFACE

The revision of hymn texts is nothing new. Hymn book editors have always applied their 'tinkering tongs' to the verbal structures of the hymns in their books. But what is presented here is something new. In the past, revision has been designed to 'improve' the texts—by eliminating doubtful theology, bad grammar, and weak expressions, as well as by introducing new thoughts which, in view of the editors, develop the hymn in a more satisfactory way, or emphasize what is implicit in the original text. Until recently such revisions have only rarely been concerned with the problem of changes in the meaning and usage of language. But in the latter part of the twentieth century we have become aware of the problems some of the old hymns present to modern worshippers.

Although a few recent hymn books, notably the *New Catholic Hymnal* (1971) and *With One Voice* (1979), have modernized some of their texts into a 'you' form, the forthcoming *Hymns for Today's Church* (1982) breaks new ground by consistently applying the principle to *all* its hymns. In this present booklet Christopher Idle explains how this policy was arrived at, why it was adopted, what the background is, and how it has been applied in this new hymn book.

It is an answer to the problem of singing the hymns of earlier generations in contemporary worship. It argues that these old hymns, as we have received them, will disappear from use simply because they are becoming unintelligible to modern Christians. But they are too valuable to be lost. Therefore they are to be rescued by the modernization of their language.

However, what begins as a question of language soon becomes a series of questions about theology, sexism, syntax, thought-form, imagery, Biblical allusion, and so on. The whole subject has many more ramifications than are dealt with here. For example, is it true that all the received texts in a 'thou' form are unintelligible and therefore unusable? Should we try to rescue a good many of the older hymns? Perhaps it would be better to let them disappear from use and clear the way for new hymn texts to be written?

Although I confess I have had hesitations about the particular answer given here, I nevertheless welcome it. This for two reasons. First, there have been many comments in various places about the desirability of such revised hymnody but, to my knowledge, this is the first presentation of the case at length and in detail. Second, the hymn book, *Hymns for Today's Church,* which is the fruit of the policy applied, will be the first to be totally consistent in having its texts in a modern 'you' form throughout.

It is not the last word on the subject. It is more in the nature of a first word of what is likely to be a continuing debate.

Robin A. Leaver

INTRODUCING—PEOPLE AND WORDS

'I will sing with my spirit' said the apostle Paul, 'but I will also sing with my mind'; that was a correction, a promise, and a resolution. It is framed in the singular; but the context of 1 Corinthians 14.15 is worship *together;* hymns are designed for congregations, but if our praise is to be real, individual members need to understand it too.

Paul no doubt sang also with heart and voice! But here it is the role of the *mind* that he is keen to safeguard, and it is a biblical principle that the words of worship should be intelligible. Sometimes in history this principle has been lost; the reformation was a period of rediscovery.[1] However unsure of its reformation heritage the church has become, in the past twenty years it has been making herculean efforts to shift its liturgies into something like the vernacular.

It has approved modern Bible translations for public use; it has battled its way towards modern-language versions of most of its services; it has found it necessary en route to update collects, creeds, and canticles. Only the hymns remain. For some people, this fact stands as a last bastion for lingering nostalgia; others argue that it is more important than this. For others, who love hymns no less, it becomes an anomaly as unhelpful as it is unnecessary; but what is hardest to change is invariably last on the list.

Just as English hymns entered public worship as a result of private pressure, so their revision is a highly unofficial activity. hymnody is still an area of free enterprise in liturgy; except in Methodism, there never was an authorized hymnal.[2] Early in 1974 a small group met to explore the possibility of a fully 'contemporary' hymn book. The music was tackled separately, and, being less contentious, needs no booklet to defend it. But we have never lost sight of the complex inter-relation of words and music when considering any hymn.

My own work has been with the words group—a team of nine with a wide variety of background, age, and temperament, united in the conviction that the gospel of Christ needs expression in good contemporary hymns. We have received invaluable help from our own and other churches, and from friends outside the group. Much of our thinking has grown or shifted as our work has progressed; in particular, we were driven to some conclusions far more radical than anything we had at first envisaged.

This booklet is an invitation to join us in our thinking, and an attempt to justify the steps we have taken to help Christians in worship. Through this personal account, a window may be opened to much wider issues; books and committees come and go, but every generation must learn to praise God with the spirit and the mind.

[1] See, e.g., Article XXIV of the XXXIX Articles of Religion, and Cranmer's 1549 Preface now printed in the BCP as 'Concerning the Service of the Church'.
[2] Not even the Baptist Union has the authorizing power of the Methodist Conference.

1. WE HAVE BEEN WARNED!

'Leave our hymns alone!'—this is the initial and natural reaction, expressed at various levels, to the news that 'they' are somehow going to change the words of well-loved and familiar hymns.

The next chapter will glance at how editors have actually behaved; but the 1906 Preface to EH puts the objection with some force:
> 'Efforts . . . to improve the work of competent authors have had the inevitable result. The freshness and strength of the originals have been replaced by stock phrases and commonplace sentiments; and injury has been done to the quality of our public worship as well as to the memory of great hymn-writers'.

Similar protests have been lodged before and since—we come to John Wesley in chapter 4—and a recent example is from Canon Frank Colquhoun's *Hymns That Live* (1980). The hymns of Mrs. Alexander, he says, 'are timeless . . . they require no editing or revising'. Furthermore, she regarded any such process as 'literary sacrilege'.[1] But when the editing of older texts goes so far as to replace archaic pronouns and verb-forms with modern ones, the outcry is intensified.

In 1966—the days of the Church of England's 'Series 2' revisions of liturgy—the then Dean of Bristol, Douglas Harrison, warned: 'Woe betide any liturgical commission which tries to put hymnbooks into acceptable modern language and into respectable theology!'[2]

At the same conference, as it happened, Dr. Stella Brook argued against the use of the pronoun 'you' when addressing the Godhead, partly because of the danger of lapsing into 'you-who'. Since then, the revision of the old collects (where the danger would be most acute) has generally managed to avoid that trap[3], and the conservatism of the sixties in some matters began to look very remote within a fairly short time.[4] Meanwhile, those churches with *Songs of Praise* had been happily singing *Lord of all hopefulness* since 1931; Jan Struther (Mrs. Joyce Placzek) was among the first to use at least 'your'—six times in this hymn—when addressing her Lord. It came so naturally that few people noticed how revolutionery it was.

An Islington Conference president, Prebendary Peter Johnston, pleaded during one annual address for 'a kind of RSV hymn book'—but even the Revised Standard Version Bible retains the old pronouns. The Roman Catholics went a stage further with their 1971 *New Catholic Hymnal* where most of the modernizations of older texts were done by one man. And the 1977 *The Australian Hymn Book* (published in Britain two years later as *With One Voice*) did a similar job, neither volume venturing to tamper with final rhyming 'thee', 'thine' or 'art', and only moving to 'you' and 'your' where this could be done fairly painlessly.

[1] *op. cit.* p.48—see below ch. 2.
[2] *Liturgical Reform: Some Basic Principles;* (CIO, 1966) p.23.
[3] Unlike the hymn, not addressed to God at all, *How firm a foundation;* its first stanza includes a 'you-who unto Jesus . . .' which the tune serves only to emphasize!
[4] That same year, Eric C. Fudge, a lecturer in Linguistics, wrote in the *Church of England Newspaper* 'No matter what *spiritual* obstacles to understanding there may be, we must see to it that there are no *linguistic* ones' (*CEN* 14.1.1966).

All this, and rumours of more to come, was enough to set off the alarm bells from those resisting such changes. In February 1975, Professor Bishop Richard Hanson pleaded in *The Times* for some truly contemporary yet poetic hymns; the Methodist Norman Goldhawk replied in a letter showing little enthusiasm for revision of language. Other Methodists were stirred up by the thought of updating Wesley in their proposed new book; and 1979 saw a number of warning shots.

The *Church Times* and the *Church of England Newspaper* published letters from at least one angry archdeacon: 'God preserve our precious heritage of English hymnody from the tinkerings of Michael Saward's team of "specialists" . . . to what purpose is this waste?'—though a glance at the context of that last phrase might give pause for thought.

The famous *PN Review 13: Crisis for Cranmer and King James* (also 1979), while concerned mainly for the Book of Common Prayer and the Authorized Version of the Bible (on which its better arguments have never been seriously answered), found room for a footnote supporting Wesley's policy of hymn-conservation: 'Those who promise to do over some two hundred of the best-loved hymns might take this admonition to heart'. And the Church Society magazine *Crossway* no. 6 (May 1982) included a fierce attack on our own 'ill-conceived and ill-prepared action'.

At a more specialist level, the Bulletin of the Hymn Society of Great Britain and Ireland not unnaturally noted the way things were going. Its editor, Dr. Bernard Massey, in a very positive review of *With Once Voice*, said:

> 'The Editors were, it seems, under considerable pressure to modernise the language. The alterations they have made are likely to be matters of some debate, at least for a while . . . [they] have used a very gentle touch . . . They have refrained from altering hymns which are classics of their kind and hymns whose poetic language is essentially unparaphrasable.'[1]

But earlier that same year Dr. Massey had written two pages arising from the 1978 *Lutheran Books of Worship* (Minneapolis), in which he was much more guarded. The alteration of hymn-texts, he says, can be 'a slippery and seductive slope'; its main danger is a resulting babel of voices where every editor is a self-appointed Bowdler, and the once-familiar hymn becomes totally unfamiliar.

Where scholars and hymnologists demur at the modernizing process, what of the bulk of the people who sing hymns? Here is an even stronger gut-reaction against change—or so it might appear. This is, after all, the true test for any theory; congregations will have the last word, because hymns are for singing, not for mere analysis.

It is here that we have been most encouraged. The readiness of a wide range of congregations to welcome our work in its earlier stages has made a great difference to its progress. Of course, the real testing is to come—and no doubt also the severest reaction. Isaac Watts discovered long ago that wherever there is innovation, there is also attack; we do not claim his genius, but we do share many of his aims.

---

[1] Bulletin No. 146 September 1979.

2. WE ARE NOT THE FIRST

At the York Church Congress of 1866, Roundall Palmer, Earl of Selborne, called attention to 'the mutilations which the original texts of some of the finest of our English hymns' had undergone. His own *Book of Praise* had set a different example by its restorations of authentic versions.

When we recall that *Hymns Ancient and Modern* was first published in 1861, and ponder the respective fortunes of the two books, we may appreciate what Michael Saward said at a Westminster Abbey 'Come and Sing' in May 1982; 'All of us are quite used to singing revisions of old hymns'.

As we survey the scope of editorial revisions, four things soon become apparent:
(a)   There is great divergence between what congregations sing, and the words originally written.
(c)   Most worshippers are not aware of this.
(c)   This divergence is largely played down by hymnal editors.
(d)   It is often hard to discover the original text.

The EH Preface has been quoted as a sample of 'purism'. Its editors do indeed print *Hark! how all the welkin rings* directly before the composite version which has replaced it, *Hark! the herald angels sing*. But they have not gone back to Wesley in *O for a thousand tongues* (formerly 18 verses beginning 'Glory to God, and praise, and love'); the stanzas are both selected and rearranged.

Something similar happens to the hymn known among Methodists as *Come let us join our friends above* and among Anglicans as *Let saints on earth in concert sing,* since EH, AMR, and AHB find the latter a more convincing opening line, and indeed drop the former altogether.[1] But even EH does not merely juggle with lines. A notable change turns *Our God, our help in ages past* to the now familiar *O God, our help . . .* Only one word, but that the first; so we avoid having three 'ours' in its opening stanza. But the author had a reason for what he did, and more recent hymnals have been bold enough to restore his original opening.[2]

So EH, while announcing itself as 'a collection of the best hymns in the English language', has a sprinkling of the little dagger-signs indicating changes—which in AHB adorn more than one in three of the hymns. And still more variants are covered by words such as 'traditional' or 'and others'.

Frank Colquhoun's comment concerned the work of Mrs. Alexander, who tends to evoke extremes of praise or blame. EH and AMR are surprisingly kind to her verses, but, of her eight hymns in AHB, four are significantly changed and two more are shortened.

[1] The reverse process operates with Bishop Mant's hymn based on Isaiah 6; Anglicans search in vain for *Bright the vision that delighted* in many Free Church books, whose compilers have dropped this difficult first stanza in favour of the next one; so the hymn becomes *Round the Lord in glory seated.*
[2] e.g. *Grace Hymns* (1975), *Christian Hymns* (1977), and *With One Voice* (1979).

No stand for textual purity, however qualified, could survive long. AMR's 1950 Preface concedes:

> 'This book does not always adhere to the original text of the hymns. The Editors of the earlier editions made alterations to meet the requirements of a hymn-singing congregation, and the present Editors see no reason to go back on the practice of their predecessors. Many of the great Charles Wesley's hymns have hardly ever been sung as he originally wrote them. Not a few authors, including Dr. Neale, have agreed that for the purpose of a hymn-book the versions of their hymns in *Hymns Ancient and Modern* were, on the whole, improvements.'

Canon Cyril Taylor has concluded that this policy of 'pastoral editing' has much to do with the genius and strength of this, the most successful of all hymnals. That aspect of revision was on the agenda of the Hymn Society Conference in 1982.

When *Songs of Praise* was published, it revealed the hand of a rather different Percy Dearmer from the one of EH; *Songs of Praise Discussed* (1933) suggests that he cannot now decide about revision. In a notable page, headed 'Improvement or Mutilation?' (p.50), he appears to be thinking aloud,

> 'Some of our most successful hymns are . . . the result of considerable alteration . . . It is the bad emendations that do harm.'[1]

The heirs to the EH tradition have taken their cue from the welcome honesty of AMR—and from common sense. The Preface to *English Praise* (the 1975 Supplement) says:

> 'The editors have not hesitated to abandon the principle adopted in the *English Hymnal* that "hymns should be printed, wherever possible, as their authors wrote them". The history of liturgy is one of change and development in the texts, and hymnody is now for us an integral part of liturgy.'

And even Dr. Erik Routley, that connoisseur of words strong and original, welcomes some revising.

> 'We have no right, nowadays, to pass over without a blushing sense of incongruity the quite unspeakable couplet
>
> > Christian children all must be
> > Mild, obedient, good as he.
>
> . . . it is time to ask that some genius alter that couplet, or at least those three objectives, to something more suitable for the praises of Christian parents'.[2]

Let that example lead us, then, to particular hymns; *Rock of ages* is one whose heyday is past—but what a heyday—It has drawn unsurpassed tributes from some who might dispute its theology and deplore the personality of its author; once it could claim to be one of the three or four most popular hymns in the language.[3] It began in a *Gospel*

---

[1] On p.116 he goes one better with a delightful paragraph on 'The Hymnic Worm'— vermicular hymns abounded in the eighteenth century, and they have all had to be cut, or simply go under!

[2] *Hymns Today and Tomorrow* (1966) p.77.

[3] In 1895 James King's *Anglican Hymnology* provided some statistical evidence for this.

Magazine article of 1775 comparing human sin to the National Debt, and concluding with a four-line verse which later grew into the hymn that we know—more or less.

Here is a classic problem of establishing an original text. Indeed, where an author is often revising (like Watts, or Toplady here) or generously accepting the suggestions of others (like Mrs. Alexander, or Neale), it is not so much the original text we seek, as the last version known to have been approved by the writer. And if this becomes our criterion, what do we make of Percy Dearmer's characteristic note on *Jesus calls us:* 'In 1871 a mutilated text in the SPCK *Church Hymns* led Mrs. Alexander to revise her work, but not for the better . . .'[1]

All editors grapple with *Rock of ages,* and they adopt varied approaches. *Wesley's Hymns* has three stanzas, including the lines 'From thy wounded side which flowed', 'Save from wrath and make me pure', 'Could my zeal no langour know', and 'In my hand no price I bring'. There is no trace of 'Not the labours of my hands', nor of other phrases we may have thought vital. But even Wesley drew the line at the earlier lines, 'Leprous, to the fountain fly' and 'When my eyestrings break in death'.

By the time of the 1933 Methodist book there are four stanzas, and eight of the 18 lines appear in a different form. In general these changes are those which have been widely accepted; until verse 4, which still offers some variables, they correspond with EH, AMR, and AHB. But the complete history of *Rock of ages* is very complex—in a hymn with some claim to be a top favourite.[2]

Other hymns of prime popularity reveal similar variety. *Eternal Father, strong to save* has a long list of variations; there is no 'received text' of even *When I survey the wondrous cross, Praise, my soul, the king of heaven,* or *Guide me, O thou great Jehovah. Lo, he comes with clouds descending* started life as

> Lo, he cometh! Countless trumpets
> Blow before his bloody sign!

—and the beautifully-constructed *Blest are the pure in heart* consists of two stanzas from Keble's original, and two by W. J. Hall!

Even if we lack the reference books, a close comparison between half a dozen hymnals is enough to establish the point: we are not the first! Anyone deliberately pursuing a policy of textual purity would produce a quite extraordinary and unusable volume, and one which would reflect a greater 'fundamentalism' than anything displayed by enthusiasts for older Bibles or Prayer Books. The fact that 'everybody's doing it' is not of itself a reason for us to follow suit; but we must be grateful for the pastoral and practical concern which has treated hymns as tools rather than tyrants. The best editors have always been motivated, not by the memory of great writers, but by the needs of Christian worshippers.

[1] *Songs of Praise Discussed,* p.134.
[2] Julian's great *Dictionary of Hymnology* unravels many of the threads; but the hymn still appears in diverse forms in books of verse claiming to represent original texts.

3. FACING THE DIFFICULTIES

It is possible to argue that there are no major difficulties in using archaic language in worship—that there is positive merit in retaining a flavour of antiquity in our hymns, which even more than prayers or readings have the added power of music to communicate far beyond any intellectual grasp of the words.

But before we put this to the test, we must face the question, What is 'today's language'? Here I venture to list some common mistakes. It is a mistake—

> to insist that there should be no specialized language at all for worship
>
> to insist that language used in worship should be a kind of 'highest common factor' of those present on each occasion
>
> to insist that newcomers should be able instantly to grasp the significance of everything that is being said or done.

So I am not arguing for 'basic English', nor for the language of ordinary conversation, the media, or the Good News Bible, as the standard for our hymns.

Many human groups have their own semi-private ways of speaking which we would not want ironed out into flat uniformity. The same group may expect to use a different vocabulary depending on context, company, mood, place, or time of day. And all of us *understand* more words than we actually *speak*.

The Christian church has a tradition of language enriched by Scripture, history, and experience; think of the 'feel' these words have in worship as distinct from their secular connotations: Jerusalem (Jordan, Lebanon . . .), grace, righteous, church, preaching, sermon, body, bread, wine, crucifixion. None of these words can be accurately 'translated' into any other English ones. None can be dropped, however liable to misunderstanding. To those who would like to see these distinctions abolished, I can only say that this is nonsense, both linguistically (since meanings cannot be controlled by dogmatic utterances), and theologically (see for example Harry Blamires *Where do we stand?* (SPCK, 1980)). When the sacred and secular are equated, in language as elsewhere, the latter invariably destroys the former.

So in hymnody: it is absurd to imagine that by filling our songs of worship with tractors, pylons, concrete, town halls, motorways, supermarkets, and council flats, we somehow bring God nearer to those who use such things.[1]

Hymns which depend on these images fade very quickly; they are also plagued with a condescending tone and a lecturing style which seems to 'do down' the worshipper, his church, and his faith, and lift up the personality of the writer.'[2]

---

[1] See also Grove Booklet on Ministry and Worship No. 12 *The Language of Series 3* by David L. Frost (1973); and Grove Liturgical Study No. 2 *Language, Liturgy and Meaning* by A. C. Thistleton (1975).

[2] See also *Hymn Society Bulletin 154* (May 1952) p.56.

Anne Ridler has argued that hymn-writers, unlike poets, must be self-abnegating; they must discipline themselves to avoid damaging the singers (and eventually boring them) and asserting themselves. A hymn should leave the congregation feeling not 'What a fine writer!' but 'What a great God!'

So certain uses of language are to be avoided; worship demands a definite *'timbre'* of Godward approach, whether we address God directly or not. But that is not the same as forming a secret language known to fewer and fewer people, describing an inner world unrelated to anything outside it. This opposite extreme has often been in nineteenth century hymnody, as well as in some imitative, pietistic, writing of the present century. When a kind of fake-antique diction adopts archaic phrases because they sound more 'holy', the offence is compounded.

We can accept the admonition of J. R. R. Tolkien not to imagine that what is new is somehow more authentic—'shake yourself out of this parochialism of time!'[1] But we need not believe either, that antiquity conveys authority; Tolkien was after all a professor of English, specializing in archaic and invented languages!

And even if we manage to avoid a banal and ephemeral style we are left with a great range of hymnody that is rapidly becoming unintelligible. It still carries (for some) an emotive resonance that must not be dismissed; but when people find it impossible to worship with the mind, it is time to look afresh at some of the hindrances.

Hymnals are still dominated by the personal pronouns and adjectives 'thou', 'thee', 'thy', 'thine', and 'ye'. Often they present no obstacle; but if they are demanded as the only proper form of address to God, it is fair to ask what Scriptural authority there is for reserving them in this way. When they are addressed not to the deity at all but to one another, or even objects, the arguments about reverence have no weight.[2]

As for obsolete verb forms ending in '-est' or '-eth', those with an academic education find it hard to believe the extent to which phrases they taken in their stride may be totally misconstrued.

Such simple (?) lines as 'can it be that thou regardest'; 'but naught changeth thee'; 'of the poor wealth thou wouldst reckon as thine', 'which wert and art and evermore shalt be', may not be understood at all. Forms such as 'shalt', 'wilt', 'wert' and 'wast' are especially problematic; sometimes the very first line of a hymn brings a mist over the sense which makes the rest difficult to appreciate: *To thy temple we repair; There is a book who runs may read; He wants not friends that hath thy love.*[3]

It is no answer to talk about dialect survivals, or about singulars and plurals; most people neither use nor understand their native tongue in this way. Anyone disputing this should try to conduct an open discussion of such hymns among ordinary Christians who know their Bibles and indeed their faith, but who left school without taking any exams.

[1] I. M. Carpenter (ed.) *The Letters of J. R. R. Tolkien* (London, 1981) p.226.

[2] e.g. 'Come, ye faithful, raise the anthem'; 'He changeth not, and thou art dear'; and (to a star!) 'Dawn on our darkness and lend us thine aid'.

[3] Perhaps: 'This man doesn't want any friends who love God'?, But if these are easy, try 'And dost thou say "Ask what thou wilt"?'

Here, then, is the first hurdle we have to overcome, partly because some find it hard to see or impossible to admit. Then comes the question of revision; the fabric of the hymn books in current use depends so heavily on this style that it is a bold step to change it. It is not simply a matter of emending verbs and pronouns; most of the examples quoted have other problems too; most also come from the nineteenth century where much of the trouble lies. Sometimes Watts and Wesley, with their firmer grasp of strong words, and less need for false archaisms, need far lighter editing than do the Victorians.

We resolved at an early stage to try to eliminate what was generally obsolete. We considered the alternative of rewriting only where no rhyme or structure was at stake. We recognized the special use of archaism in legal or ceremonial contexts; we did not feel that this constituted sufficient reason to persist in singing hymns the language of which no longer communicated their original meaning.

In addition to pronouns and verbs, we faced a phalanx of obsolete conjunctions, relatives, and prepositions ('unto', 'where'er', 'whosoever', etc.) and with some few exceptions resolved that these also had to go—together with nouns and adjectives which had lost their meaning or had it changed by use or association.

The Son of God his glory hides/With parents mean and poor no longer means what it says: 'care' is now normally used in a good sense rather than meaning a burden of anxiety; the verb 'own' usually means 'possess'—consider *I'm not ashamed to own my Lord* and others. The study of semantic change is vast and fascinating; but it must not be confused with what we think words ought to mean, or wish they did. Even the best dictionaries cannot keep pace with the spoken word; 'gay' and 'bleeding' are two recent casualties. We no longer use 'bowels' to mean 'tender compassion', and the last century could sing more freely (in church!) of bosoms and breasts than ours can. It is an anachronistic error to blame the writers for expressions which now sound merely comic; if they had seemed so at the time, they would not have been printed so frequently.

A further problem is that of Bible references. To someone knowing his 1611 version, the hymn book presents few difficulties of this kind; but can today's worshippers pick up allusions to the 'great Desire of nations', the 'man of sorrows', or even to 'I know that my Redeemer liveth', all of which have changed in modern translations? 'Zion' is deeply embedded in Scripture, but now caries other connotations. Should we still sing of Bethel or Canaan? We have no desire to rob hymns of a wealth of biblical pictures; liturgical tradition is likely to keep alive the 'Alleluias' and 'Hosannas' which have disappeared from the Good News Bible. Chapter 6 describes how we tackled some of these questions.

Unlike Bible translators or liturgical commissions we are handling metrical rhyming verse. All revisers must have an ear for rhythm; those who bring prose up to date are however free to create new patterns of stress and sound. We had no such choice; rather, the responsibility of working within a tight framework and a given scheme. But before coming to details, we need to face some very strong objections. We are not the first revisers; but have we gone too far?

4. MEETING THE OBJECTIONS

There are five arguments used against modernizing.

(a) The literary objection

Dr. Samuel Johnson was not thinking primarily about hymns, to be sure; but no-one could have put it better:

'An author's language, sir, is a characteristical part of his composition, and is also characteristical of the age in which he writes. Besides, sir, when the language is changed, we are not sure that the sense is the same.'[1]

In many situations, he is surely right. If I study Shakespeare I do not want an edited, shortened, or updated, version; I want to hear him speak as he spoke then, and I must make the necessary adjustment from my conversation to my book.

So I have quoted Johnson exactly as Boswell relates him. But I could quote the same sentences, but omit the final syllable from the word 'characteristical'. (An early biography of Eric Liddell called him an 'internationalist'; we would call him an 'international' because that now expresses what D. P. Thompson meant, and the older word now means something different. *And our concern would probably be with Liddell rather than with Thompson*).

In literary editions of Malory, Langland, Chaucer, or even Milton, we can read their original spelling and vocabulary. But when they are quoted in *The New Oxford Book of English Verse*, several concessions are made to the non-specialist reader; school editions are even simpler.

If editors state openly how they have proceeded, there can be no objection to making older texts clearer by modernizing the language. Our duty in hymnody is not to authors but to 'this congregation here present'; not to the original phrase but to the truth it originally conveyed.

It would be very odd to treat hymn-writers more reverently than we treat our greatest poets. And if authors change their own hymns, why should their work be suddenly 'frozen' by their deaths?

Henry Kirke White, who wrote *Oft in danger, oft in woe* (or rather, originally, *Much in sorrow, oft in woe*) died at the age of twenty-one; it is hardly likely that, had he lived, he would have left his youthful scribble entirely unaltered. And scribble it was—ten lines on the back of a mathematics paper. Would he mourn that only three of these lines survive today? And should we sing what even Milton wrote at the age of sixteen, word for word?[2] This is no reason for rewriting Keats or Wilfred Owen; but it is part of the argument for making hymns more usable.

The whole trouble with the literary argument is that it proves far too much. We could never again sing Dearmer's *He who would valiant be* (which transforms Bunyan); Herbert's *Let all the world in every corner sing* would not escape; and Wesley himself would prove indigestible.

It is because we love the old hymns that we do not want to lose them; if we cannot revise, the whole body of classic English hymnody would gradually but surely shift from the parish church into the local library.

[1] Boswell *Life of Johnson* (OUP, 1970 ed), p.308.

[2] In fact nobody does; musicians insist that *Let us with a gladsome mind* be made singable.

(b) The cultural objection

In 1961, Malcolm Muggeridge wrote in his diary: 'Almost the only thing the English never lose their faith in is hymns.' Literary objections are concerned with textual precision; cultural ones go deeper.

When *O God, our help in ages past,* or *Eternal Father, strong to save,* is sung at a memorial service, or *Once in royal David's city* on Christmas Eve, or *Abide with me* at Westminster or Wembley, there is a particular feel to the old hymns that is part of our national heritage.

In defending the Prayer Book and the Authorized Version, writers like David Martin and Bryan Morris make the point well. It does not take much to damage a masterpiece. So Professor Martin says 'If a man is capable of messing about with greatest words in the English liturgy he could do it to Shakespeare;'[1] Bryan Morris offers a spoof version of *Abide with me:*

'Stay with me; evening approaches rapidly . . .'[2]

He says this is easy to do—and we believe him! It is so easy that few of our own critics can resist the temptation to demonstrate this curious art. But it is a rather different task from the one we have attempted.

The hymns quoted in this section have all retained in our versions their openings, their structure, their classic and greatest lines, and by far the bulk of their vocabulary. We would want the originals to be accessible, but this is not the function of a church hymn book. And we applaud C. H. Sisson, also quoted by Brian Morris, who says (p.123) 'There is no such thing as passing on profound truths in superficial speech.'

Those who edit hymn books have no standard text before them. We are not translating a single masterpiece but coping with a diverse collection of texts by hundreds of writers and in a state of constant flux. And, we want to say that the Victorians too could be superficial!

The cultural objectors could have a field day, if they chose, when they reach no. 325 in our book. *God save our gracious queen.* Here, if you like, is a real kite-flyer; we have tried to make the anthem more credible, and have no idea how seriously anyone will take it. Few now sing 'Frustrate their knavish tricks' and the absolute monarchy presupposed here has begun to grate for many loyal but thoughtful citizens. But even these words were once new-fangled!

(c) The congregational objection

A nagging question when we started was 'Is this what congregations really want?' Even if we could justify changes on other grounds, fellow-Christians might turn their back on our work as some had to Tate and Brady's 'New Version' of the Psalms in 1696.

It is one thing to debate theories, or recite new words or old in a mock sing-song voice; it is quite another the use them in church. We have learned in practice a number of things:

The more mobile our society becomes, the more variety Christians are likely to find as they travel around.

[1] In Brian Morris (ed.) *Ritual Murder* (Carcanet, Manchester, 1980), p.13.
[2] *op. cit.* p.71.

Church members have shown remarkable resilience in adapting to change. If congregations are still intact after moving from the Prayer Book to Series 2, then Series 3, and now the Alternative Service Book—all in the space of fifteen years—new hymns will not break them.

Where minimal changes are made, they take them in their stride. When 'Open thou the crystal fountain' becomes 'Open now . . .' few even notice.

Where larger alterations are needed, and the reasons explained, many people are grateful—'So that's what it means!'

And we have received from such practical testing a volume of useful comment and response—pointing out a weak revision, suggesting a better emendation, or even demanding that we should be still more radical: 'If you change this, why not that?' Some who initially found the idea of modernizing hard to accept, have come to see the strength of the case for it. It is not from congregations that the opposition has been coming.

(d) The Wesleyan objection

It is given that name because it is so famous; it is used a great deal to oppose any editing at all. So we must quote it again—from the Preface to the 1779 edition of *Wesley's Hymns,* written (be it recalled) when he has seventy-six:

'Many gentlemen have done my brother and me the honour to reprint many of our hymns. Now they are perfectly welcome to do so, provided they print them just as they are. But I desire they would not attempt to mend them; for they really are not able. None of them is able to mend either the sense or the verse. Therefore I must beg of them one of these two favours; either to let them stand just as they are, to take them for better or worse; or to add the true reading in the margin, or at the bottom of the page; that we may no longer be accountable either for the nonsense or the doggerel of other men.'

If there are two hymn-writers able to claim that no-one could possibly improve their work, it was the brothers Wesley; Charles the greatest of them all, and John, whose paraphrases have lasted outstandingly well, and who was the more disciplined writer, sometimes checking the over-enthusiastic flights of his gifted brother.

But could these words be justly applied to any other authors—to Bonar, or Bunyan, or Montgomery? John Wesley, certainly, would never have used them of Watts, whose life overlapped with his own.

John, in fact, was no Wesleyan in this matter; he found the Watts version of the hundredth Psalm inadequate because of its fatal opening stanza:

'Sing to the Lord with joyful voice,
Let every land his name adore;
The British isles shall send the noise
Across the ocean to the shore.'

So he boldly abandoned that verse and redrafted Watts' verse 2 to produce *Before Jehovah's awful throne.* It is not unreasonable, two centuries later, to change that 'awful' to 'awesome', and thus to follow Wesley's example rather than his precept.

As for the latter-day Wesleyans, when items from the new Methodist book were introduced in Westminster Abbey in May 1982, five of the eight Wesley hymns were sung in a form diverging from their originals. The complete list for the 1983 book includes first lines with the tell-tale 'alt. J.W.' So, however bad Wesley's contemporary 'menders' may have been, this objection is not what it seems; as so often, the great evangelist was trying to have his cake and eat it.

Let us call an altogether humbler witness; John Ellerton, author of one great hymn and many good ones, also suffered editing in the late nineteenth century. His response was equally characteristic:

> '. . . anyone who presumes to lay his offering of a song of praise upon the altar, not for his own but for God's glory, cannot be too thankful for the devout, thoughtful, and scholarly, criticism of those whose object it is to make his work less unworthy of its sacred purpose.'[1]

(e) The theological objection

This final protest is not the argument for retaining whatever theology the original hymn contained. It is that we sin against the truth by altering what others have set down of their experience of god. We gladly record the findings of fellow-pilgrims; we may question these, but not distort or corrupt them.

To this there is a double reply. First, that Scripture is the final arbiter of all our human gropings, findings, and assurances. This is to simplify a long debate, but it accurately reflects evangelical Christianity.

The second answer comes from the Bible itself. When the Epistles quote the law, or the Gospels the prophets, or when the New Testament quotes the Psalms (the Hebrew hymnal) they do not use an exact text.

Watts himself noted this fact, for a slightly different reason:

> '. . . in Luke 19.38 the disciples assume a Part of a Verse from the 118th Psalm, but sing it with Alterations and Additions to the Words of David. The other is the Beginning of the second Psalm, sung by Peter and John and their Company, Acts 4.23, 24, etc. You find there an Addition of Praise in the Beginning . . . Then there is a narration of what David spoke, "who by the Mouth of thy Servant David hast said," etc. Next follow the two verses of that Psalm, but not in the very words of the Psalmist . . .'[2]

Watts here is proving more that we aim to; even Scripture is re-worded to bring out or enrich the meaning of the original. There is plenty of evidence of liturgical borrowing and development.[3]

We are not dealing with uniquely-inspired texts. We make no change lightly, but we cannot treat hymns as holier than the Scriptures—nor as more sacred than those who sing them.

---

[1] See John Whale *One Church, One Lord* (SCM, 1979), pp.137-141. Ellerton's hymn *The day thou gavest* is itself based on an earlier anonymous work.

[2] From 'A Short Essay Toward the Improvement of Psalmody'—appended to *Hymns and Spiritual Songs* (1707).

[3] 'His mercy endureth for ever' (AV!)—but not the way in which it is expressed.

5. THE ALTERNATIVE

We have already hinted several times at the alternative to updating the texts of older hymns. It is so vital that it must be spelled out unmistakably.

If no revisions are made, even of currently-acepted texts, hymns will soon represent a quite different world from the rest of our worship, let alone from that outside. In many churches, everything else has made a major step towards twentieth-century language. It will prove a difficult matter to have to change gear three or four times in each service, and step back into the past.

The next stage is that hymns become the preserve of the specialists. Their texts will not be lost; bookcases will contain them, but no longer at the back of the church. Scholarly research will preserve the best; some of the others will be collected for their quaintness in a spirit of folksy nostalgia—along with records of early jazz, old steam trains, or the street cries of London.

But hymns as a congregational experience, an expression of what we want to sing to God, 'the response of the redeemed community'—all this will be quietly lost as each item in turn becomes unusable through some fatal phrase or ridiculous word—ridiculous only because no living language stands still, and new meanings will wreck the old verses.

J. D. Douglas complained in a recent article 'Where are the hymns of yesteryear?'[1]; the answer is that nowadays fewer publishers have the nerve to print them, fewer clergy to choose them, and fewer congregations to sing them.

There is a fountain filled with blood is a magnificent hymn marred by imagery which now looks unacceptably exaggerated. It is being printed less and less, and consequently sung less and less. In spite of its many beauties, *The God of love my shepherd is* (George Herbert's version of Psalm 23) is not surviving well—largely because of 'Or if I stray, he doth convert/And bring my mind in frame'. Will Henry Williams Baker's *The King of love my shepherd is* follow it into oblivion because of its fifth verse, with 'thy unction grace bestoweth' and 'transport of delight'? A glance through the section on 'Heaven' in the older hymnals will show a host of once-popular hymns which themselves have passed through the pearly gates. What will take their place? Only the hymns of today and tomorrow—but the door will be left wide open for the shoddy, the trendy, and the smart; if the traditional hymn no longer speaks for us, we will find other forms of song which do.

Of those hymn books which have aimed above all at purity and conservation, some have made history in their own way, but few have carried conviction among active Christians. If hymns are to remain an integral part of Christian worship, we can no longer avoid the need for thorough editing, including modernization where necessary.

[1] *Church of England Newspaper* 29 January 1982.

6. THE BOOK TAKES SHAPE

Quite apart from the work done by individual members (drafting, re-drafting, experimenting) and in churches and conferences (singing, assessing, discussing), the words group for *Hymns for Today's Church* has met together over seventy times, mostly over a full day and including several residential conferences.

From the beginning we planned a book which retained a solid corpus of traditional hymns, while including the best from the 'hymn-explosion' of the past twenty-five years. Of a preliminary list of some 300 established items, three-quarters finally made it to the book; but all through the years until the last deadline, we were receiving new texts (all assessed anonymously) and having second and third thoughts about old ones. We took seriously every responsible plea from outside the group to include or omit particular hymns; in the end, virtually every item was selected on a clear majority vote of this group of nine.

We made an early decision to remove 'thee', 'thou' etc., from the main book. Rather than have a fresh debate at every hymn, we made this a basic working principle. The main problem it posed was with rhyming lines ending in 'thine' (including the frequent 'thine'/'mine' rhyme), and the even more frequent final 'thee'. The verb-form 'art' had also proved to be an over-convenient rhyme for 'heart'; this created difficulties which we have tried in various ways to overcome. We have allowed a single 'untrue' rhyme; in *How sweet the name of Jesus sounds;* 'Weak is the effort of my heart' is followed by 'but when we see you as you are'.[1] But the hardest example of many 'thee' rhymes came in H. E. Hardy's verses, *O dearest Lord, thy sacred head,* depending as they do on a consistent rhyme of 'me'/'thee', with no room for manoeuvre.

But even if rhymes and syllables can be managed, the consonants in 'thou' 'thee' and 'thine' add a strength that is missing from 'you' and 'yours'. *Thine be the glory* is a better first line than *Yours be the glory* (some books have even gone for 'Yours is . . .'); 'How great you are' is not so firm a refrain as 'How great thou art'. The former of these we include, the latter not.

Another early decision on principle was the omission of the title 'Holy Ghost'. It occurs nowhere in any Bible version since 1900; nowhere, as it happens, in the ASB 1980, except (ironically) in the hymn *Come Holy Ghost,* and in the canticles reprinted from the Book of Common Prayer. The main difficulties this meant were the need to provide and alternative to Thomas Ken's doxology (which we have done, set alongside the old); and the first line of *Gracious Spirit, Holy Ghost,* which becomes *Holy Spirit, gracious guest.*

But altered first lines are exceptional. Poems often have titles other than their opening phrase, but hymns are known by their first lines; so we kept *Jesus shall reign where'er the sun* and *All people that on earth do dwell,* in spite of their archaisms. But we drew the line at

---

[1] In *Love divine* we have 'glory'/'adore you': perhaps no worse than the original 'glory'/'before thee', more liberty being accepted for rhymes that do not conclude a stanza.

'gladsome', 'begotten', and 'awful'; where the first line has been changed, a cross-reference in the index makes the hymn traceable. Expressions such as 'O', 'Lo', 'Hail', 'Hark', and 'Ah', caused much debate[1]; in the end we retained most of them somewhere. This is not 'everyday language', but such words are intelligible signals of a heightened emotional awareness in singing God's praise.

We also discussed a range of words like 'magnify', 'abound', 'bless' (meaning 'praise'), 'own' (meaning 'confess to'), 'foe,' 'slay', and so on. There is no possibility of absolute consistency; every hymn has its own mood and style, and we tried not to shatter this with an alien expression. 'Hundreds slain by desert foe' could still be a credible press headline; the words are often understood, but used in a way one stage removed from naturalness.

Where such vocabulary is vital to the structure or strength of a hymn, it is kept; where it obscures the meaning, it goes. And nobody got his or her own way all the time, and no book would satisfy anyone in its entirety. Some would have preferred to keep 'O *magnify* the Lord with me'; others were reluctant to retain 'Stand up and *bless* the Lord'. Wherever possible, we aimed at the 'invisible mending'[2] technique, in which a similar sound or stress causes the least possible disturbance to the flow of a hymn. Thus we made such changes as:

Fill thou my life	—Fill now my life
Seek thou this soul of mine	—Seek out this soul of mine
And the city's crowded clangour	—and the city's crowded clamour
For such a worm as I	—for such a one as I
poor and mean and lowly	—poor and meek and lowly
Unbosom all our cares	—unburden all our cares

Sometimes we have changed the stress to make a line easier to sing; 'bruising the serpent's head' becomes 'and crushed the serpent's head'—a change which strengthens the powerful imagery, and is consistent with Genesis 3.15 (New International Version). There are common 'hiccups' of stress in *God is working his purpose out, All creatures of our God and king,* and even *For all the saints,* which are now healed; those who question our right to do this are reminded that what we sing as 'and prove your good and perfect will' was originally 'And prove thine acceptable will'.

Sometimes a number of difficulties are met at once. Isaac Watts has:

'Bless'd be the Lord, who comes to men
With messages of grace;
Who comes in God his Father's name
To save our sinful race.'

Here is an awkward stress, a bad rhyme, and some sexism of which Watts was blissfully unaware. We offer instead, to solve all three:

'Blessed be the Lord, who freely came
to save our sinful race;
he comes, in God his Father's name,
with words of truth and grace.'

[1] 'Lo' actually occurs in the text if this booklet's predecessor in the Grove Worship Series (No. 80, p.13).

[2] A happy phrase attributed to Archbishop Donald Coggan.

But this raises the question—should we yield to the strong pressure (mounting even more rapidly in America) against the generalized use of 'men' and 'mankind', 'sons' and 'brothers'? We resolved that often we should. We had enough sympathy with the anti-sexist lobby to want to remove thoughtless stumbling-blocks to Christian worship—though not enough to be ruthless, and certainly not enough to reduce god the Father to a heavenly 'parent'.

Like our contemporary Brian Wren, we went through our own earlier work, sometimes reviving the word 'humankind', with which Dryden and John Mason Neale both felt at home. But 'person' is not an attractive word; sometimes 'Christian' will serve for 'brother', but maybe a future and more radical editor will take this further than we have done.

A similar feature of some older hymns is 'blackness' used (without Scriptural foundation) as a symbol of sin, death, or hell. This can cause deep hurt, and is eaily changed—as is the word 'leper' which no leprosy worker would now use, and which the World Health Organization banned long ago.

Like others before us, we found many sentiments which Victorians found helpful but we think unhealthy. We reacted against the exaggerated modesty (let alone the precious language and poor rhyme) of

> 'May his beauty rest upon me
> As I seek the lost to win;
> And may they forget the channel,
> Seeing only him.'

This now becomes:

> 'May his beauty rest upon me
> as I seek to make him known;
> so that all may look to Jesus
> seeing him alone.'

As for *Lead us, heavenly Father, lead us* which (accidentally, it seems) uses the word 'dreary' of the Son of God, we try, like the *New Catholic Hymnal*, to do some mending of our own.

Many hymns see the church building as a temple, unlike the New Testament which regards God's people as his new and living temple. We faced this in *Christ is made the sure foundation:* first the old, then the new:

'To this temple, where we call thee	'We as living stones invoke you
Come, O Lord of hosts, today . . .	come among us, Lord, today . . .
And thy fullest benediction	and the fulness of your blessing
Shed within its walls alway.'[1]	in our fellowship display.'

But another famous example of the dominance of buildings may stand for many more: old and new again—

'We love thine altar, Lord;	'We love the holy feast
O what on earth so dear?	where, nourished by this food,
For there by faith adored	in faith we feed on Christ,
We find thy presence near.'	his body and his blood.'

[1] The last line of the old version enshrines a bonus giggle; like another classic from the same hymn; 'Bridal glory round her shed'!

The first is a static, un-Anglican, and furniture-centred verse, with a strained participle for good measure—not to mention the unhappy 'O what on earth . . .?' The second stresses the meal, in strong sacramental terms and in an active and biblical mode.

In chapter 4 we mentioned biblical allusions—how far have we gone to accommodate them? We saw no reason to demand a knowledge of 'Judah's seer'; but 'Death of death' and 'hell's destruction' are firmly enough established to be positively desired. Some of the newer hymns are bold with names; Timothy Dudley-Smith clearly expects some response of heart and mind to 'Eden indeed is with us yet', or 'to make of life's brief journey/a new Emmaus road'.

But what about the 'Stem of Jesse's rod'? We kept open a corner for some hymns which might still be needed in traditional (we do not say 'original') form. By the end, there proved to be seven of these. Ken's doxology, *The Lord's my shepherd, Come Holy Ghost,* and the 2-verse National Anthem, need no justification. The others may seem more surprising; *All hail the power of Jesus' name,* because the insistent rhymes with 'all' make it hard to modernize faithfully (so 'Jesse' can stay put!)[1]; *And can it be,* because we had not satisfied ourselves that we had done justice to this Wesley tour-de-force; and the hybrid *He who would valiant be*—because Michael Saward's strong adaptation is an even longer way from *Pilgrim's Progress.* But *Who honours courage here* deals sexism another mortal blow; it stands with the modern-language versions of this group, available for bolder spirits to sing.

Have we been consistent? Of course not! We have tried to keep faith with original authors and periods wherever possible, to the Scriptures and today's church always. The hymns of George Herbert, conceived in such love and faith, preserved by accident, never sung in his lifetime, remain an enigma; with one exception we came to doubt that they were properly viewed as hymns at all. Fine, tender, moving poems they are; but that is not our purpose.

Our book includes some new items of special interest, published here for the first time; the solemn *O Trinity, O Trinity* paraphrased from the Greek Orthodox tradition; a new version of the Compline hymn *Before the ending of the day,* and of the yet more ancient 'Phos hilaron' which comes into ASB only in archaic versions; a paraphrase of the earliest known hymn in English, Caedmon's *Now praise the Protector of heaven;* and a bold successor to Thomas Carlyle in Michael Perry's version of Luther, *God is our fortress and our rock.* And many more!

Sometimes we were thwarted by copyright restrictions; some publishers declined to allow emendations. We have been enormously encouraged by writers such as David Mowbray who have responded very graciously to constructive criticism of previous texts, and George Caird who revised his own published translation, *Shepherds came,* to meet the principles to which we were working.

We have filled some notable gaps in the available range of hymns, particularly on baptism, the life of Christ, the Holy Spirit, mission, healing, work, and the arts. There is still much, much more to be done.

[1] *Songs of Praise Discussed* says of this hymn 'the best tribute we can pay is to transfer it from the 18th to the 20th century. This we have tried to do' (p.235).

APPENDIX: COMMENTARY ON SELECTED HYMNS

(a) Amazing grace

This hymn was omitted from from many books between the 1861 *Hymns Ancient and Modern* and the 1960s; largely because of two popular recordings, the tune has become widely known and has carried the words along with it. Recent hymnals have often included it, and it remains in wide demand. The original text is easily accessible in the 1979 facsimile reprint of the *Olney Hymns*.

> 'Amazing grace—how sweet the sound—
> that saved a wretch like me!
> I once was lost, but now am found;
> was blind, but now I see.'

Only the punctuation has been changed in this opening verse; we dispense with brackets and (as always) prefer lower case at the beginning of a line. The syntax is a little unusual, but the meaning is clear.

> 'God's grace first taught my heart to fear,
> his grace my fears relieved;
> how precious did the grace appear
> the hour I first believed!

Newton wrote . . . ' 'Twas grace that taught my heart to fear'. Since this hymn is often sung by people who have little idea what (or even who!) 'grace' is, our new first line makes it clearer, while at the same time removing the archaic 'Twas . . . ' but retaining the vowel sound. Line 2 is a change consequent on this, from 'and grace'.

> 'Through every danger, trial and snare
> I have already come;
> his grace has brought me safe thus far
> and grace will lead me home.'

Newton's first and third lines were: 'Thro' many dangers, toils and snares/'Tis grace has brought me safe thus far.' We have put 'snare' in the singular to make a more adequate rhyme—which in turn meant writing 'every danger . . .' rather than 'many dangers'. 'Toils' then meant traps, and was almost a synonym for snares; 'trials' fits the context, is biblical, and in sound similar enough to 'toils' for the change not to be widely noticed. 'Toils' today suggests hard work, which may be true but was not Newton's point. 'His' in line 3 removes the archaic ' 'tis (again retaining the vowel sound), and more importantly stresses the fact that 'grace' is not an independent power, but an action and attribute of God. Although archbishops have traditionally been referred to as 'his grace' we felt that this obsolescent usage should not prevent us speaking of the grace of God in this way today.

> 'The Lord has promised good to me,
> his word my hope secures;
> my shield and stronghold he will be
> as long as life endures.'

We retain the strength of the original first line, and the second in spite of its awkward inversion, after some experiments in clarification. But line 3 read 'he will my shield and portion be'; 'portion' is no longer used in this sense, and has humorous connotations, so it is replaced by the biblical 'stronghold'. At the same time, the harshness of the inversion is lessened. The force is now that *this* is what he will be, rather than that he *will* certainly be this.

> 'And when this earthly life is past
> and mortal conflicts cease,
> I shall possess with Christ at last
> eternal joy and peace.'

Newton's fifth verse ran 'Yes, when this heart and flesh shall fail/And mortal life shall cease/I shall possess within the vail/A life of joy and peace!' The first problem is 'vail'—a reference to the AV of Hebrews 10.20. But the reference is brief and unexplained—veiled indeed!—and we are unprepared for it; furthermore, even the RSV drops the word 'veil' and no subsequent translation revives it; so in spite of the truth in Newton's biblical image, we resolved to drop it. The other changes are largely consequent on that one; 'past' in line 1 to rhyme with 'at last' in line 3; 'life' in line 1 to remove the suggestion of heart-failure(!), and the insertion of 'conflicts' in the third line—which like the previous 'trial' and 'stronghold' is a word which Newton could well have used.

But should the hymn end here? Newton concluded with a stanza found in very few books: 'The earth shall soon dissolve like snow/The sun forbear to shine/But God, who called me here below/Will be for ever mine.' The 'snow' image is of doubtful suitability, and the third line (echoing Drake's drum?) sounds odd today. We are persuaded that verse five ends sufficiently well for it to conclude the hymn; the tune is normally a slow one, and five verses are enough. The verse starting. 'When we've been there ten thousand years' which has often been attached to the hymn, is not by Newton, and introduces ideas foreign to both the author and to Scripture.

(b) Hark! a trumpet-call is sounding

Here is a hymn with a history of variants in its very first line, and one which raises questions of translation. Sometimes we have recaptured original meanings lost in this process (as with the 'Veni Creator'); but we are convinced that our first duty is to the worshippers, our second to the English-language author, who has created a new text rather than a translation, and only then to an original foreign-language writer—unless it is a Scripture paraphrase, where we have invariably given the original its full weight.

> 'Hark! a trumpet-call is sounding,
> "Christ is near," it seems to say;
> "Cast away the dreams of darkness,
> children of the dawning day." '

So, why a trumpet-call? 'Vox clara ecce intonat' says the sixth century (this and many other original-language texts are given in the *Historical Companion to Hymns Ancient and Modern* (published by Wm. Clowes in 1962)); Caswall wrote 'Hark! an awful voice is sounding', but 'thrilling' arrived three years later and came to stay. But if it is indeed a thrilling voice, why is it not clear, but merely 'seems' to say something? We chose to keep 'seems' and to introduce the biblical image of the trumpet, which in a passage such as Revelation 4 'seems' indeed to speak. 'Nigh' has been replaced with 'near'; we judge that the 'magic' of the older word is probably spurious—surviving indeed in dialect, but paradoxically making Christ seem rather less near! We decided the other way on 'cast': 'throw away' would have been banal in a way that 'near' is not, and 'cast' is more in use today than 'nigh' is.

Finally, in this all-important first verse, 'ye' had to go from the last line, and the gap allows us to introduce the vividness of 'dawning' with a sense of movement and growing hope.

> 'Wakened by the solemn warning
> let the earth-bound soul arise;
> Christ, her sun, all harm dispelling,
> shines upon the morning skies.'

The only change here is 'harm' for 'ill'; the phrase 'all ill dispelling' is excessively labial, and none too clear. For some time our text read 'gloom', which fits the 'sun' imagery; but to dispel 'harm' is a mightier work, and true to the original 'ut tollat omne noxium'.

> 'See! the Lamb, so long expected,
> comes with pardon down from heaven;
> let us haste, with tears of sorrow,
> one and all to be forgiven.'

The initial 'Lo' is the only loss from the version in present use. We felt that 'Hark' is allowable, 'Lo' not—and in any case a first word had stronger claim for support than one lower down in the hymn.

> 'That, when next he comes in glory
> and the world is wrapped in fear,
> with his mercy he may shield us,
> and with words of love draw near.

> 'Honour, glory, might and blessing
> to the Father and the Son,
> with the everlasting Spirit,
> while eternal ages run.'

All this is unchanged.

(c) Let saints on earth together sing

This is a Charles Wesley hymn known to Methodists as *Come, let us join our friends above;* as no. 949 in *Wesley's Hymns*, it has five 8-line stanzas. We concur with those Anglican books (EH AMR AHB etc) who find the original first line inadequate—possibly too open to parody, certainly having a quaint feel to it. But we are reluctant to drop Wesley's first four lines entirely, so have reinstated them as the final stanza.

> 'Let saints on earth together sing
> with those whose work is done;
> for all the servants of our king
> in earth and heaven, are one.'

23

Let saints on earth in concert sing has become a familiar first line. But 'concert' now carries some quite irrelevant connotations—and is in any case not what Wesley wrote. The original runs: 'Let all the saints terrestrial sing/With those to glory gone'. Our new first line has both clearer sense and New Testament echoes, while for our second we accept an established line as superior to the earlier quaintness.

> 'One family, we live in him,
> one church above, beneath,
> though now divided by the stream,
> the narrow stream of death.'

Exactly as Wesley, except 'live' for 'dwell'—a change in line with all recent Bible versions. 'Dwell' is intelligible but archaic, and has no advantage over 'live'.

> 'One army of the living God,
> to his command we bow;
> part of his host have crossed the flood,
> and part are crossing now.'

Unchanged; the moving and simple use of a biblical image commonly applied to death. Following this verse we omit much of Wesley, in common with other editors. By modern standards the old hymn is too long to retain this mood, and includes many phrases that simply sound strange today—'and we expect to die . . . with wishful looks we stand . . . our old companions in distress . . . and greet the blood-besprinkled hands . . . and land us all in heaven.'

> 'But all unite in Christ their head
> and love to sing his praise:
> Lord of the living and the dead,
> direct our earthly ways!'

A new stanza which we trust is in harmony with the spirit of the older ones, and provides the essence of what was expressed in the discarded words; in particular, the unity of heaven and earth in Christ, and the way that our meditation (as in Wesley and often in the Psalms) turns into a direct ejaculatory prayer. This verse also introduces the name of Christ—absent from the original—and describes him in words from Romans 14.9.

> 'So shall we join our friends above
> who have obtained the prize;
> and on the eagle wings of love
> to joys celestial rise.'

So we end with Wesley's opening words, slightly adapted from 'Come let us join' and 'that have obtained'. We have lost the parallel of 'celestial/terrestrial'; but retained the biblical images of the prize (Philippians 3.12-14) and the eagles' wings characteristically glossed with 'love'; and gained a strong final line (Exodus 19.4).

CONCLUDING—CHURCHES AND SONGS

In the third century AD, a certain heretical bishop found it necessary to suppress a number of hymns sung in honour of Christ. The grounds for his action? 'They were new, and the work of new men!'[1] New approaches, new hymns, and new writers, will always meet some resistance. But if this generation survives long enough, there are many great hymns yet to be written by it.

Our close attention to the text of the traditional hymns has alos convinced us that they are worthy of the highest respect. This is true above all of the unsurpassed talents of Isaac Watts and Charles Wesley; one, the classic-majestic; the other, the dogmatic-ecstatic.[2]

As a student of language rises from a study of Shakespeare with renewed admiration for the craftsmanship of the man who has already thrilled him in the theatre—and then returns to see and hear the plays again—so we have found the best hymn-writers as convincing in our long committees, or late-night sessions with dictionary and commentary, as they are in the joyful, transforming experience of corporate Christian worship. Many of them were also humble; we have the more reason to be. But like them we believe we have received a gift to be shared with all God's people. Dr Erik Routley says that if a hymn 'distracts the congregation from the act of worship by obscurity, by irrelevance . . .', or by anything else, 'it fails'. He adds:[3] 'A hymn, then, is not really a good hymn until it has been written, well chosen, and well sung'.[3] So let it be: Amen!

[1] Paul of Samosata, Bishop of Antioch 260-270, quoted by C. S. Phillips in *Hymody Past and Present* (SPCK, 1937) p.21.
[2] This latter expressive phrase is quoted from elsewhere by Canon A. M. Allchin.
[3] *Hymns and Human Life* (John Murray, 1952) pp.298-9.